story
WORKS ™

HOW STORIES CAN ADVANCE YOUR BUSINESS, CAUSE AND CAREER.

SHARLENE SONES

WWW.BRANDSTORIA.COM

"The most successful brands in the future will master storytelling in a way that is compelling to consumers, media and other key constituents and Sharlene Sones delivers that message very effectively in *Storyworks*. Every marketer should apply her insights and observations to the brand narrative they are developing and evolving moving forward."

— Mark Beal, *Managing Partner, Taylor*

"A fun and imaginative look at the realm of story marketing. The book is short, pithy, and full of gems. Read this book, and you'll connect the dots on why storytelling is such a hot business trend."

— Michael Margolis, *Author,* Believe Me: a Storytelling Manifesto for Change-makers and Innovators

"*Storyworks* will help you understand how to get more value from your branding and marketing. Because stories do work, whether you're trying to network for your career or connect with customers — story is the "special sauce" that creates meaningful connection for fans. And an added bonus: the book's design provides a real treat for the left side of the brain, too."

— Raf Stevens, *Corporate Storyteller, Author of* No Stories, No Fans.

"The longest and hardest nine inches in marketing is the distance between the brain and the heart. *Storyworks* uncovers a basic truth about that journey and how we provide context for meaning. We connect emotionally through the power of storytelling. Sharlene Sones provides the roadmap to leverage the power of narrative as a cornerstone for brand and business success."

— Stan Phelps, *Author of* What's Your Purple Goldfish? How to Win Customers and Influence Word of Mouth

What's it all about?

GUIDING PREMISE:

A PRIMARY BUSINESS OBJECTIVE:

GROWTH

FANS
FAITHFUL
BELIEVERS
COMMUNITY
TRIBE

(THE UBER-BELIEVERS WHO WILL PROPEL YOUR BRAND, YOUR PRODUCT, YOUR SERVICE)

ADVOCACY
CONNECTION
LOYALTY
BUZZ

but the

"How to"

can seem elusive

STORY IS THE ANSWER

STORYTELLING IS A CORNERSTONE OF BRAND & BUSINESS SUCCESS

Maximize

YOUR BRAND

THROUGH THE USE OF STORY AS A
PRIMARY STRATEGIC ASSET

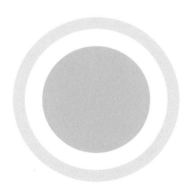

FINDING THE MEANING AND VALUE IN YOUR BRAND

AND PUTTING IT TO WORK.

CONNECTING THE HEAD
with the heart
OF YOUR CUSTOMERS

———

"THE MOST DIFFICULT AND IMPORTANT DISTANCE
FOR A BRAND TO BRIDGE"
- STAN PHELPS, 9 INCH MARKETING

———

Impacting

STICKINESS

THE EMOTION EVOKED IN STORY IMPROVES
RECALL, RETENTION AND OVERALL STICKINESS.

Attracting
CUSTOMERS

BY PRESENTING A STORY IN WHICH PEOPLE CAN SEE THEMSELVES.
WELCOMING THEIR PARTICIPATION IN SHARED NARRATIVE.

NOW SERVING:

THE WHOLE STORY

I shop (along with legions of others) at Whole Foods.

Their brand story — starting with their first all-natural and organic food store in Austin, TX — is a complement to my lifestyle. The Whole Foods story is, effectively, part of my own story: a shared narrative for living a lifestyle that is "whole" — healthy, organic and kind to the earth. And a story supported by buying and consuming the products they offer. And they keep my trust and loyalty by continuing and expanding upon this role in my life story through their blog, The Whole Story.

You need only look at a few food brands in the store to find more examples of more stories that impact why we buy. Some of my favorites include Annie's Homegrown salad dressings; Newman's Own snacks (if I'm going to eat a cookie, theirs are way better than an Oreo, right?) and Tom's of Maine natural personal care products (minty fresh toothpaste without the harmful chemicals). Each company's products are supported by the unique story of their founder and a basic desire to fill a need: doing good and making good. I trust that their products are what they claim to be, based not just on their reputation, but also on the integrity and strength of their story. Using these products enables us - as consumers - to participate and have a role, too. And doesn't that feel good?

THE BOB'S RED MILL STORY

If you're having breakfast with me, you might have a bowl of steel cut oatmeal. And if you did, it'd be made with Bob's Red Mill. What I love about Bob's: there really is one! And his story represents the integrity and honesty that makes me believe in him and his products.

Here's the story that "got" me and countless others to start buying Bob's Red Mill.

Long before there was a Bob's Red Mill, Bob picked up a book on old stone-grinding and became fascinated with the traditional milling process. It was a moment of serendipity that wouldn't fully play out for decades. After retirement, Bob was taking an afternoon walk when he stumbled on an old mill that was for sale. The memories flooded back, enticing him to purchase what he saw as a beautiful red mill waiting to fulfill old dreams. He quickly built a successful business producing nutritious flours and cereals through the timeless process.

When a fire burned the building to the ground a decade later in 1988, Bob felt he "owed" family, friends & employees to rebuild. His commitment to people as well as a quality product is why I love the brand – and why I trust that every bowl of oatmeal will live up to its promise: nutritious, high quality cereal made with old-fashioned ideals and values.

IF YOU REMOVE

The Story

—

WHAT'S THE IMPACT ON YOUR BRAND?

—

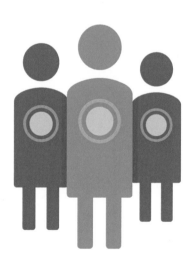

ISOLATION

WHAT YOU GET

IS A BUSINESS

WITHOUT ITS

———

WHY? PEOPLE DON'T JUST
BUY A PRODUCT OR A SERVICE.

———

THEY BUY A STORY.

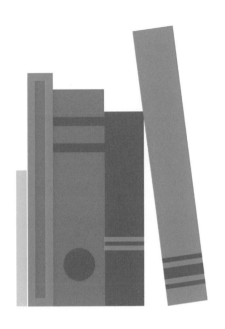

YOUR UNIQUE STORY

HAS POWER!

PUT IT TO WORK.

REASON ONE

MUCH MORE THAN ENTERTAINING SOUND BITES, STORIES PLAY IMPORTANT AND POWERFUL ROLES IN OUR LIVES.

REASON TWO

STORIES PROVIDE CONTEXT FOR MEANING; HOW WE VIEW OUR LIVES AND OUR RELATIONSHIP TO THE WORLD AROUND US.

LEADERS

OF ALL

KINDS

ENTREPRENEURS

C-SUITE EXECUTIVES

CHANGE MAKERS

JOB SEEKERS

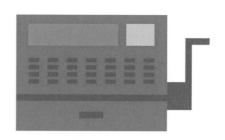

SMALL BUSINESS OWNER

PROVIDING SUPPORT

FOR CHANGE.

IMPACTING YOUR EFFECTIVENESS

TO LEAD & MANAGE.

CREATING A POWERFUL FORM OF

BRAND EXPRESSION.

GIVING PEOPLE ANOTHER REASON TO

CARE ABOUT YOU.

SECTION ②

THE
BRAND
And
STORY
MASHUP

DEVELOPING A MORE EXPANSIVE
FRAMEWORK FOR TODAY'S BUSINESS

CREATING A COMMON UNDERSTANDING OF

2 FREQUENTLY MISUNDERSTOOD AND LIMITED CONCEPTS

THE COMMON UNDERSTANDING:

BRAND AS A NOUN

AN IDENTITY

(sort of like saying all you are is what you wear)

* The red bottle is a registered trademark of The Coca-Cola Company; the swoosh is a registered trademark of Nike, Inc.

A BEHEMOTH

CORPORATE ENTITY

(AND A PRACTICE RESERVED FOR
BIG GUNS WITH BIG RESOURCES)

CONSIDER A MORE EXPANSIVE FRAMEWORK:

We're
ALL BRANDS

WHETHER YOU'RE AN ESTABLISHED ORGANIZATION,
A FLEDGLING START-UP OR THE OUTSOURCED
EMPLOYEE WHO'S RAISING A NEW FLAG AS
ENTREPRENEUR OR CONSULTANT:
WE'RE ALL BRANDS THAT REPRESENT A
PROMISE OF THE VALUE WE'LL DELIVER.

BRAND

―

INTERSECTION OF YOUR PROMISE
and
PEOPLE'S EXPECTATION.

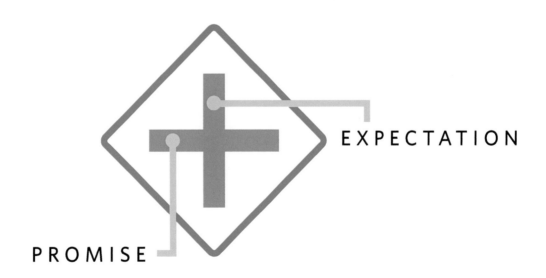

PROMISE

EXPECTATION

not just a manual that sits on a shelf...

—

BRANDING AS A VERB

—

"What you do"

WITH

"What you stand for"

A REPUTATION MANAGEMENT SYSTEM

A BLUEPRINT FOR HOW YOU OPERATE

DEFINING, MANAGING & DELIVERING VALUE & MEANING

HELPING YOU DELIVER AN EXPERIENCE

THAT REINFORCES CORE VALUES

———

ON BRAND
ON STRATEGY

———

CREATING A PLATFORM AND AN ENVIRONMENT FOR YOUR

POTENTIAL
TO THRIVE

STORY  CULTURE

informs

"BRAND IS A
lagging indicator
OF CULTURE."

- TONY HSIEH

Story **2b**

STORIES ARE HOW WE

CONNECT

TO THE

WORLD

A HOW WE FILE, RETRIEVE, & REMEMBER INFORMATION.

B FORM OUR DEEPEST VALUES & BELIEFS

C SHAPE SELF IDENTITY

IT'S HOW WE'RE

HARD WIRED

The Neuroscientists

SAY IT'S SO.

NEUROLOGICAL

EVIDENCE THAT INDICATES STORYTELLING IS FUNDAMENTALLY
THE WAY OUR BRAIN PROCESSES INFORMATION INTO MEANING.

TRUTHS

—

YOURS,
YOUR STAKEHOLDERS,
CUSTOMERS
AND PROSPECTS

STRUCTURE:

A A BEGINNING, MIDDLE & END

B A HERO

C AN INCITING INCIDENT

D A CHALLENGE/OBSTACLE TO OVERCOME

E A LESSON THAT INFORMS BEHAVIOR

BUT OUR COMMON

"Once Upon a Time"

———

UNDERSTANDING OF STORY
CAN MUCK UP THE POINT.

———

BRANDS CAN EMPLOY VARIOUS

FACETS *of* STORY

IN WAYS FAMILIAR TO BUSINESS

VIGNETTES

ANECDOTES

METAPHORS

CASE STUDIES

PRESENTATIONS

TESTIMONIALS

LEVERAGING THEM AS

"A DISTRIBUTION CHANNEL

AND MECHANISM

for meaning."

- ANNETTE SIMMONS

The Mash-Up 2c

CONSIDER TWO KINDS OF
BRAND STORYTELLING

Ⓐ THE BACK STORY

YOUR BACK STORY. THE BACKWARD LOOKING HISTORY AND STORY THAT INFORMS "WHO YOU ARE." BRAND ACTS AS AUTHOR AND "TELLER."

Ⓑ DYNAMIC STORIES*

PLAYING YOUR STORY FORWARD. THE LIVING STORIES THAT ARE CO-CREATED WITH CUSTOMERS AND STAKEHOLDERS. BRAND ACTS AS PARTICIPANT AND ENABLER OF CONVERSATION.

* The Coca-Cola Company. (2012). Coca-Cola Content 2020. Two part videos created with The Cognitive Media available at http://www.youtube.com/watch?v=LerdMmWjU_E and http://www.cognitivemedia.co.uk/index.php/blog/category/our-work

The

"WHY I DO, WHAT I DO"

NARRATIVE THAT MAKES YOU
TRUSTWORTHY & BELIEVABLE.

BEHIND
EVERY BRAND
IS A
GREAT STORY

informs

A BACK STORY OF
RELEVANCE AND MEANING

LOGOS, CAMPAIGNS AND
MESSAGING THAT CONNECT

A SOURCE FOR FINDING
& REVEALING YOUR
CORE VALUES, ESSENCE,
& PURPOSE.

—

WHAT YOU STAND FOR

—

THE LL BEAN STORY

The "Down Maine" outdoor apparel & equipment company was founded by namesake Leon Leonwood Bean when he developed and sold a unique boot to hunters, created after he returned from a hunting trip with cold, damp feet. Seeking a more functional boot, he called on a local cobbler to stitch leather uppers to workman's rubber boots. Created and sold from in his brother's Freeport, ME basement, L.L. marketed his "Maine Hunting Shoe" or the "Bean Boot" to non-resident hunting license holders, reaching out to them through direct mail including a money-back guarantee. When 90% of the initial production proved defective L.L. made good on his promise, honoring returns and then making improvements that would become a New England and nationwide standard for generations. Quality, reliable products made for a hunter, by a hunter. Today, their guarantee remains as a backbone of the LL Bean's brand along with a thriving catalog-based business. The bean boot? It's a timeless, quintessential classic celebrating its 100th anniversary.

Stand

FOR SOMETHING

OR YOU'LL FALL FOR ANYTHING.

- GINGER ROGERS

CREATING & EXPRESSING VALUE, MEANING, SIGNIFICANCE

IN PEOPLE'S
LIVES THROUGH
A STORY THAT
RESONATES
AND INVITES
PARTICIPATION

Why DO YOU CHOOSE

THE CAR YOU DRIVE?

WATCH YOU WEAR?

SMARTPHONE YOU USE?

WHO YOU DO BUSINESS WITH?

WE'RE ALL FROM *Venus* WHEN WE MAKE MOST PURCHASES

——

BEHAVIORAL SCIENTISTS REVEAL
OUR DIRTY LITTLE SECRET:
BY & LARGE WE ACT...
THEN RATIONALIZE IT LATER.

——

BUT THERE MAY BE SOMETHING ELSE GOING ON...

PEOPLE BUY BASED ON HOW THE BRAND FITS WITH THEIR PERSONAL STORY, INFORMING SELF-IDENTITY

BRANDING U: CONSIDER PEOPLE'S RELATIONSHIP TO THEIR COLLEGE
"I'M A HARVARD MAN" (OR A PENN OR BABSON WOMAN)

A DEFINING ELEMENT OF

THE PURCHASE PROCESS

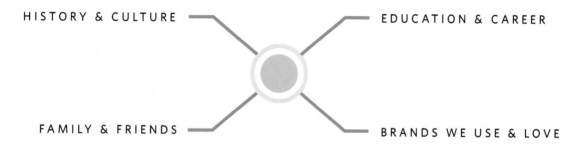

HISTORY & CULTURE   EDUCATION & CAREER

FAMILY & FRIENDS   BRANDS WE USE & LOVE

A BRAND SUCCESS SITS AT THE INTERSECTION OF A SHARED NARRATIVE WITH YOUR CUSTOMER'S STORY. **B** YOUR STORY BECOMES THEIR STORY, AND VICE VERSA

Ⓑ DYNAMIC STORYTELLING:

Actively, intentionally and purposefully

ENGAGING STORY WITH AND BETWEEN PEOPLE

YOUR CUSTOMERS, PROSPECTS, INFLUENCERS, STAKEHOLDERS.

IGNITING
CONVERSATION

CENTRAL TO MARKETING, PRODUCT
DEVELOPMENT AND INNOVATION

RESPONDING TO A NEW CLIENT-CENTRIC
WORLD REQUIRES NEW SKILLS IN

STORY LISTENING

and

STORY SHARING

MARKETER AS CONNECTOR

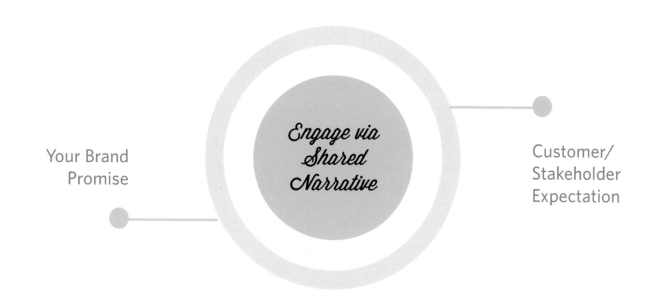

Your Brand Promise

Engage via Shared Narrative

Customer/ Stakeholder Expectation

DR. PEPPER'S MILLION DOLLAR TUITION GIVEAWAY

Dr. Pepper created a campaign to give away $1 million in college tuition to "change the lives of students across the country." The challenge: submit a video story online to explain why they deserve the prize. The stories were captured in two ways: a video team from Dr. Pepper traveled to campus during the collegiate football season recording students on site, while students also submitted them online. Selected finalists participated in events at the AT&T Cotton Bowl Classic half-time and also featured their personal stories on limited edition Dr. Pepper cans.

The result? Dr. Pepper was the enabler of the stuff of dreams -- helping people continue their academic and personal pursuits. They provided a platform for shared narrative with all the students, not just the winners, inviting them into a story to convey their unique purpose & role in life.

BUILD SYSTEMIC CAPABILITIES IN

Storytelling

"DEVELOPMENT OF INCREMENTAL ELEMENTS OF A BRAND IDEA - CONTAGIOUS IDEAS RELEVANT TO BRANDS, BUSINESS OBJECTIVES AND CUSTOMER INTERESTS - THAT GETS DISPERSED SYSTEMICALLY ACROSS MULTIPLE CHANNELS OF CONVERSATION FOR THE PURPOSE OF CREATING A UNIFIED AND COORDINATED BRAND EXPERIENCE."*

Source: The Coca-Cola Company. (2012). Coca-Cola Content 2020. Two part videos created with The Cognitive Media available at http://www.youtube.com/watch?v=LerdMmWjU_E and http://www.cognitivemedia.co.uk/index.php/blog/category/our-work

SECTION ③

joy
OF
CONVERSATION ™

AS BRAND CHEF WE'RE CALLED

TO SET THE TABLE &
SERVE A *Feast*

THIS REQUIRES A DIFFERENT TWIST ON SOME FAMILIAR

INGREDIENTS & METHODS OF "COOKING"

THAT CONNECTS PEOPLE TO EACH

OTHER THROUGH *conversation*

PEOPLE,

ESPECIALLY MILLENIALS,

DON'T WANT TO:

"like you"

FRIEND OR TWEET

ABOUT YOU...

THEY WANT A SPOTLIGHT
ON THEMSELVES
THEIR OWN LIVES AND
THOSE AROUND THEM.

—

NOT SOME BRAND TRYING TO SELL THEM SOMETHING.

NEW RECIPE:

FOR BRAND SUCCESS

FIRST INGREDIENT:

Find the joy

IN SHOWCASING

other people's story

YOU WOULDN'T HOST A DINNER PARTY AND MONOPOLIZE
THE CONVERSATION, WOULD YOU?

Give your "guests"
CENTER STAGE,
HIGHLIGHTING AN OPPORTUNITY
to talk about themselves

———

Ⓐ IT'S NOT ABOUT YOU, IT'S ABOUT THEM **Ⓑ** REQUIRES MOVING FROM BRAND-CENTRIC STORYTELLER TO A ROLE AS "ENABLER" OF CONVERSATION **Ⓒ** GIVING PEOPLE A PLATFORM TO SHARE THEIR STORY

HOW IT IS:

TRADITIONAL "PUSH"

MARKETING MINDSET.

ME-FOCUSED. BROADCAST.

INTRUSIVE. BRAND-FOCUSED.

TALKING AT: CONFIRMING

AN IDEA OR AGENDA.

SOLITARY/INDIVIDUAL.

THINLY VEILED SELLING.

WHAT COULD BE:

LEARNING & DEEP MEANING.

"GIFT." COLLABORATION,

CREATION, "SPARK" OF NEW IDEAS.

RELATIONSHIP. SHARING.

RELATING. REALLY HEARING.

SPEAKING WITH, NOT AT.

CONNECTION & ENGAGEMENT.

THE
NEW CURRENCY
IS
Conversation

A PRECURSOR TO RELATIONSHIP BUILDING AND AN IMPORTANT INGREDIENT FOR LEVERAGING TECHNOLOGY AS A REAL-TIME BRANDING PLATFORM

BUT DON'T CONFUSE
THE MEDIUM WITH THE
MESSENGER

MARKETING IS ABOUT
Relationships

MEET YOUR NEW HEAD
OF SOCIAL MEDIA:

YOUR CUSTOMER

"CONVERSATIONS AMONG THE MEMBERS OF YOUR MARKETPLACE *happen whether you like it or not.* GOOD MARKETING ENCOURAGES THE RIGHT SORT OF CONVERSATIONS."

- SETH GODIN

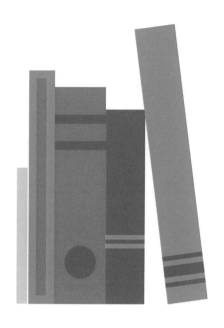

BRAND STORIES ARE
CONVERSATION STARTERS

THAT FACILITATE SHARING AND CONNECTION

GIVING PEOPLE

SOMETHING TO TALK ABOUT

successful brands:

- **A** HELP FACILITATE SHARING OF IDEAS
- **B** BUILD CAPABILITIES IN LISTENING
- **C** ACTIVELY GENERATE CONVERSATION

SKITTLES: MOB THE RAINBOW

As part of their "Experience the Rainbow" campaign, Skittles brings people together to create flash mobs that deliver kindness and love, aka the "rainbow experience," to those who don't ordinarily receive it.

Their first effort: an outpouring of valentines to a parking enforcement officer. Encouraged by Skittles, fans sent over 40,000 valentines to the officer through the mail on their own or via the Skittles site.

A great conversation starter with the focus on Skittles as enabler for random acts of kindness.

SECTION ④

story

DIFFERENTIATES

"I REALIZED THE IMPORTANCE

of having a story today

is what separates companies.

PEOPLE DON'T JUST WEAR OUR SHOES,

THEY TELL OUR STORY."

- BLAKE MYCOSKIE, CEO, TOM'S SHOES

YOUR BRAND POSITION SHOULD

Set You Apart

———

WE'RE IN HOT PURSUIT OF SUSTAINABILITY, CONSIDERING THE CRITICAL QUESTION: WHAT'S YOUR COMPETITIVE ADVANTAGE?

FINDING A REALLY DISTINGUISHABLE & UNIQUE POSITION IS DIFFICULT

AND A SUSTAINABLE ONE IS EVEN MORE RARE

BUT A POWERFUL

BRAND STORY

WILL SET YOU APART

—

IT IS UNIQUELY
Yours, AND *Only Yours*.

AND WHILE COMPETITIVE ADVANTAGE MAY
BE FLEETING, YOUR STORY CAN BE LASTING

QUESTION: IF YOU REMOVE

The Story

WHAT'S LEFT OF YOUR BRAND?

COMMODITY

BOTH SELL COFFEE

BUT DIFFERENT ISN'T ALWAYS *Better.*

REMEMBER GERBER SINGLES FOR ADULTS?

HARLEY DAVIDSON PERFUME?

SMITH & WESSON MOUNTAIN BIKES?

(NEITHER DO I).

DIFFERENTIATION WITHOUT A CONSISTENT, BELIEVABLE
BRAND STORY = A BUSINESS GONE ASTRAY

SPORTING GOODS BRANDS

PROVIDE GREAT EXAMPLES OF
POSITIONING MADE CREDIBLE
BY A BRAND STORY

NIKE = PERFORMANCE FOOTWEAR = founder and avid runner Bill Bowerman innovates by making a homemade "waffle sole" in his garage for better traction

SPALDING = AUTHENTIC ALL-AMERICAN SPORTS HERITAGE = creator of the first basketball in Springfield, MA

PRINCE = PERFORMANCE ENHANCING TENNIS EQUIPMENT = inventor of the first oversized tennis racquet, made famous when 16 year old professional Pam Shriver advances to the final of the US Open

REVEALING A
ROADMAP FOR
Potential

———

THESE POSITIONS,
SUPPORTED BY THEIR STORIES,
INFORM WHAT KINDS OF
PRODUCTS AND SERVICES
WE'LL BELIEVE...AND ACCEPT...
FROM THE BRAND.

IF YOU COVER UP YOUR LOGO ON YOUR AD, WEBSITE, BROCHURES OR THE NAME ON YOUR RESUME

———

DOES IT STILL CONVEY WHAT'S REALLY UNIQUE ABOUT YOU?

(Are you positive?)

WHY WE FAIL TO CONVEY
WHAT MAKES US *Special*

A WE THINK PEOPLE ARE
ALREADY IN THE KNOW

B WE'RE TOO CLOSE (AND
CAN'T SEE THE FOREST)

C MIRRORS HAVE DISTORTION

D BRAGGING ISN'T BECOMING

DIFFERENTIATION
BUZZ KILLERS

—

BUSINESS/INDUSTRY SPEAK

ENTHUSIASTIC, PROTECTIVE MANAGERS

DRINKING THE KOOL AID

THE KITCHEN SINK

IVORY TOWERS

DESIGN BY COMMITTEE

Have you APPLIED FOR A JOB LATELY?

THE NEED TO STAND OUT,

DIFFERENTIATE,

AND DEFINE YOUR VALUE

IS PARAMOUNT

THE RESUME IS NOT DEAD

(But it sure does stink)

THE DIFFICULTY: IT'S HARD TO CONVEY THE REAL "YOU" IN A FORM. A BULLETED LIST CAN'T CONVEY YOUR REAL VALUE AND EXPERIENCE.

IT ONLY COMES TO LIFE WHEN YOU COMBINE IT WITH YOUR STORY.

YOUR STORY =

An indispensable tool

FOR SUCCESSFUL INTERVIEWS

―――

HELPING YOU ANSWER TRICKY QUESTIONS

CONVEYING THE VALUE YOU BRING

THE KEY TO UNDERSTANDING WHO YOU ARE

& HOW YOU CAME TO BE

NOT JUST A LIST OF ACCOMPLISHMENTS

―――

SECTION ⑤

story
SELLS

WHAT ARE YOU REALLY SELLING?

—

IT'S PROBABLY NOT WHAT YOU THINK

—

It's not

JUST ABOUT THE PRODUCT/SERVICE,

but also

SELLING YOUR BRAND AS A TRUSTED, CREDIBLE SOURCE

———

THAT YOU'LL MAKE GOOD ON YOUR PROMISE
DELIVERING AN EXPERIENCE THAT LIVES UP TO THE
EXPECTATION TIME AND TIME AGAIN

GUIDING PREMISE:

It's

HUMAN NATURE

TO DO BUSINESS WITH PEOPLE WE TRUST.

WANT TO BECOME
A TRUSTED AUTHORITY?

THE STORY YOU TELL CAN
PROVIDE SUPPORT & CREDIBILITY

Ⓐ PROVIDING THE RATIONALE FOR HOW YOU CAME TO BE

Ⓑ REVEALING THE UNDERLYING VALUES OF YOUR BUSINESS

BE-
LIEVE
ME

- MICHAEL MARGOLIS

TRUST
ME

- STEPHEN COVEY

The beauty of your story

IT CAN REMOVE THE NEED TO SELL

GETTING PAST RESISTANCE, DOUBT AND MISTRUST WITHOUT SENDING SMOKE SIGNALS THAT YOU'RE "SELLING SOMETHING" OR HAVE AN AGENDA

IF YOU CAN TELL A STORY THAT
OTHERS IDENTIFY AS THEIR OWN

—

THE NEED TO
Persuade, Convince, or Sell
PEOPLE ANYTHING
DISAPPEARS

- MICHAEL MARGOLIS

THAT'S WHY

STORY SUPPLIES THE ULTIMATE COGNITIVE SALES PITCH.

Have to sell to

AN ENGINEER, BEAN COUNTER, CFO?

STORY
TRUMPS
DATA

- JANET GRECO, TRANSITION ONE ASSOCIATES

DATA = OPEN INVITATION TO CHALLENGE *(just because we can)*
BUT YOUR STORY IS YOUR STORY. REFLECTING PERSONAL
EXPERIENCE AND MORE DIFFICULT TO CHALLENGE.

NUMBERS DON'T *Resonate*

THEY ARE FLAT, UNEMOTIONAL, FACELESS.

———

BUT CONNECTED WITH STORY

They Come Alive

CONVEYING MEANING.

INVITING PARTICIPATION,

ACTION, ENROLLMENT

THE SAUCONY SALES TEST

THE STORY FORMULA FOR SELLING
STOP PITCHING, START STORYTELLING

I CAN SELL SAUCONY RUNNING SHOES, BLINDFOLDED.

I learned their story 20 years ago, while working over college break in a sporting goods store.

Faced with the need to help customers make sense of a huge wall of shoes and armed with a pile of specification sheets and technical data from the competitors... Saucony provided me with a memorable and meaningful story that was easy to share.

Their shoes were designed for women, by a biomechanics specialist who just happened to be a female athlete. She understood the need for special fit and construction based on the unique shape of a woman's foot (which i can still elaborately repeat today).

Lesson? Give us the behind-the-scenes "why this was created" story, providing context and meaning for your shiny bells & whistles.

"BUT I'M NOT A SALESPERSON" YOU SAY?

EVERYONE SELLS

---

a product, service, or idea

SELLING BY *any other* NAME:

NETWORKING LEADING

EXTENDING AN INVITATION TO DO
BUSINESS WITH YOU; THAT YOU OR
YOUR IDEA CAN ADD VALUE

A well told story can also

FETCH A HIGHER
PRICE POINT

CONSIDER WHAT THE AMERICAN PICKERS KNOW:

A PRODUCT WITH A STORY SELLS

AN ANTIQUE CHINA CUP = $25

MY GRANDMOTHER'S CHINA CUP,

A GIFT FROM MY MOTHER = PRICELESS

SECTION ⑥

story
INSPIRES

"MOST EXECUTIVES

Struggle to Communicate

LET ALONE INSPIRE."

- ROBERT MCKEE

WITHIN YOUR STORY IS:

A POWERFUL FORCE

FOR

Inspiring

A RANGE OF EMOTIONS, IDEAS, ACTIONS

FOUND IN THE:

"WHAT MADE YOU"
MOMENTS

———

PIVOTAL TIMES OF
OVERCOMING CHALLENGE
OR COMING TO
A REALIZATION

———

EXPOSING YOUR VULNERABILITIES, PROVIDING SCENARIOS IN WHICH PEOPLE CAN SEE THEMSELVES AND RELATE

Giving PEOPLE ANOTHER REASON TO BELIEVE & TRUST *You*

Inviting People INTO A BIG IDEA AND/OR WAY OF LIVING THROUGH A STORY IN WHICH THEY CAN PARTICIPATE

A BRAND "THEME" THAT REPRESENTS A COMMON, SHARED NARRATIVE

THE INVITATION TO EMPOWERMENT

THE LANCE ARMSTRONG FOUNDATION
"UNITES, INSPIRES AND EMPOWERS PEOPLE AFFECTED BY CANCER."

Livestrong leverages the inspirational story of cyclist Lance Armstrong, who overcame almost unfathomable odds to beat cancer and go on to win the tour de france.

His story, underscores the value of having and going after dreams, no matter how big. By sharing his story, Lance can inspire others to achieve the seemingly impossible in their own lives, too. The invitation: to re-write and edit both your own story and others impacted by cancer.

* Livestrong and the yellow Livestrong wristband are trademarks of the Lance Armstrong Foundation.

CHANGE AGENTS:

TELL ME A GREAT STORY AND

YOU'LL BE *Amazed* AT WHAT I CAN DO

OFFER UP A NARRATIVE
THAT PAINTS A PICTURE FOR A
DESIRABLE FUTURE IN WHICH
I CAN SEE MYSELF

A JUST DO IT STORY CAN

Move Us

[1] TO BUY A $100+ PAIR OF RUNNING SHOES [2] GET OFF THE COUCH [3] CHANGE HABITS AND BEHAVIORS [4] CONSIDER (AND DO) A MARATHON [5] CHANGE OUR LIVES [6] HELP OTHERS DO IT TOO

BECAUSE REASON ALONE MAY NOT BE ENOUGH TO CREATE ACTION OR CHANGE

(OR PEOPLE WOULDN'T SMOKE, EVERYONE WOULD EXERCISE AND WE'D ALL LOSE THAT EXTRA 10 POUNDS)

A Bulleted List:
NOT INSPIRING

IMAGINE IF MARTIN LUTHER KING, JR. STOOD BEHIND A PODIUM AND READ HIS "I HAVE A DREAM SPEECH" FROM A BULLETED POWERPOINT PRESENTATION

MANAGER
OF PEOPLE

ASK YOURSELF

Would you rather be coerced **or** *inspired?*

AT THE CORE OF THIS THINKING:

WE'RE ALL IN IT FOR SOMETHING MORE

THAN JUST PUNCHING A CLOCK

WE DESIRE LIVES OF PURPOSE AND MEANING

GREAT LEADERS - AND GREAT BRANDS - CAN HELP

PEOPLE REALIZE THEIR POTENTIAL, THEIR STORY

And

INSPIRATION IS

contagious.

VIRAL MARKETING IS ABOUT
PROVIDING PEOPLE WITH A
STORY WORTH SHARING

LIFE IS GOOD®

SPREADING THE POWER OF OPTIMISM

When John & Bert Jacobs' t-shirt business was practically bust in the early 90's, they found themselves "desperately searching for answers to keep the dream alive." It was found hanging on their apartment wall in the form of a smiling stick figure named Jake, whose "contagious grin, simple as it was, seemed to express everything the Jacobs brothers believed in." It was a sentiment apparently shared by others: their first printing of 48 shirts was a runaway success at a street fair by noon. In the decade that followed, life was, indeed, good. The brand realized tremendous growth through more than 900+ different products at retail across the globe, all inviting people into a "glass is half full story" epitomized by Jake's simple messge of optimism, delivered with a large dose of humor and humility.

* The character Jake and the phrase "Life is Good" are registered trademarks of Life is Good, Inc.
http://www.lifeisgood.com

SECTION 7

story
CLARIFIES

LEADERS DON'T JUST
MAKE PRODUCTS AND
MAKE DECISIONS.

―

LEADERS MAKE

Meaning

- JOHN SEELEY BROWN

THOSE YOU SEEK TO INFLUENCE ACT FROM WITHIN THEIR OWN STORIES. THEY ARE AUTHORS AND MAIN CHARACTERS IN SEARCH OF VALUE SATISFACTION

—

OFFER THEM A MORE *Powerful Story* FOR DOING SO.

- JANET GRECO

CLARIFY

WHERE WE'RE GOING AND
HOW WE'LL GET THERE
WHAT'S EXPECTED OF PEOPLE
WHAT'S IN IT FOR US,
FOR YOU, FOR ME
WHY YOU SHOULD CARE:
VALUE & MEANING

THEY CAN HELP PEOPLE UNDERSTAND
WHAT TO DO BY PROVIDING A

READY TO CONSUME "EXPERIENCE"

THAT THEY CAN APPLY TO THEIR
OWN SITUATIONS AND USE AS

A Beacon

FOR UNDERSTANDING WHAT BEHAVIORS
ARE HELPFUL AND APPROPRIATE

IN WHICH THEY CAN
PARTICI-
PATE

AND

LEARN

What we can learn from

JESUS THE STORYTELLER

HE USED STORY AS A MEANS TO REVEAL AND CLARIFY THE MEANING OF HIS TEACHINGS - BECAUSE THEY WORK

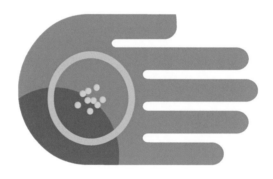

DESIGNED TO MAKE PEOPLE THINK
TAPPING INTO EVERYDAY, COMMONPLACE THINGS &
SITUATIONS TO HELP PEOPLE UNDERSTAND & LEARN

"The Mustard Seed Parable"

JESUS USES A TINY SEED AS AN ANALOGY TO CONVEY THE GROWTH GOD'S KINGDOM WOULD EXPERIENCE. EVERY PERSON OF THE TIME WOULD HAVE KNOWN THAT THE TINY MUSTARD SEED WOULD GROW INTO A MASSIVE, UNSTOPPABLE WEED THAT WOULD OVERTAKE ANY GARDEN

THE LESSON WAS DELIVERED IN THE CONTEXT OF A STORY THAT PEOPLE OF THE TIMES WOULD EASILY UNDERSTAND AS A MEANS TO DEMONSTRATE POTENTIAL

OUR BUSINESS PARABLES

DRAW ON THE SAME PRETENSES

YOUR IDEAS AND INTENTIONS
CAN BE BETTER UNDERSTOOD
WHEN PEOPLE RELATE THEM
TO THEIR OWN EXPERIENCES.

THE CULTURE BOOK:

CLARIFYING WHAT IT MEANS TO BE

THE BRAND STORY.

Zappos, the uber-successful online retail brand, published a "culture guide" written by employees. **In it, they provide 90+ pages of short stories about what the Zappos culture means to them and why it matters.**

It's a snapshot of the Zappos story brought to life. **Providing clarity to what's usually a lifeless corporate mantra. The mission is real, meaningful and understandable. Real values in action.**

Source: 2010 Culture Book, Zappos. See: http://www.zapposinsights.com/culture-book

SECTION ⑧

story
ALIGNS

IT'S ALSO SHAPED BY THE PERCEPTIONS AND VIEWPOINT OF

Others

EMPLOYEES STAKEHOLDERS
CUSTOMERS PROSPECTS
INFLUENCERS INVESTORS

DEFINED &
DELIVERED

BY THE PEOPLE WHO WORK FOR AND WITH YOU,
IN WHAT CAN BE OR SEEM LIKE IRRATIONAL GLORY

THEIR STORIES *Are* YOUR REALITY

———

"WE DON'T HAVE THE RESOURCES"

"OUR BUDGET ISN'T BIG ENOUGH TO WIN"

"THE COMPETITION IS JUST TOO STRONG"

"LEADERSHIP DOESN'T REALLY WANT TO CHANGE"

"THERE IS NO CLEAR PLAN FOR GROWTH"

ARE THEY ALIGNED TO

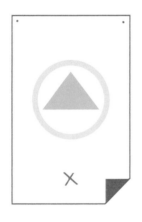 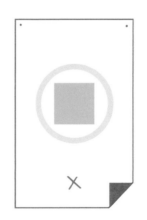 

YOUR STRATEGY?

The Story Gap

THE DIFFERENCE BETWEEN

YOUR DESIRED STORY

and

THE ONE(S) REALLY

BEING TOLD

FAILURE

TO MIND THE GAP CAN HAVE SERIOUS CONSEQUENCES. FOR YOUR BRAND, A POTENTIALLY FATAL FLAW

SIMILAR TO THE DANGER LURKING FROM A
FAILURE TO MIND THE GAP ON LONDON'S TUBE,
STEPPING SAFELY OVER THE GAP BETWEEN TRAIN
AND PLATFORM

—

YOUR JOB:

Relentessly

FIND AND WORK TO

CLOSE THE GAPS

WHAT DO YOU REALLY WANT FROM THE PEOPLE WHO INFLUENCE *Your Success?*

"BUY-IN" OR "ON-BOARDING" IS MORE ABOUT WANTING PEOPLE TO JUST AGREE WITH YOU. WHEN YOU ASK FOR FEEDBACK DO YOU REALLY, REALLY WANT IT?

F YOU WANT TO INFLUENCE THEM

TO BUY, FOLLOW OR BELIEVE

CONSIDER

Their STORY

REAK-
AST

-PETER DRUCKER

URE

RI-

THE STORY GAP *Revealed:*
WHAT DOES CADILLAC STAND FOR?

CAD 4 LIFE

5 DIFFERENT PEOPLE RESPOND WITH 5 DIFFERENT ANSWERS:

Ⓐ MY GRANDPARENTS' CAR

Ⓑ GAS GUZZLER Ⓒ ELVIS

Ⓓ BIG, FLOATING BOAT-LIKE RIDE

Ⓔ HIP-HOP URBAN

WHAT CADILLAC SAYS:

THE NEW STANDARD OF THE WORLD

SECTION ⑨

story

HUMANIZES

TO KNOW PEOPLE
WE MUST KNOW
their story.

———

- DAN P. MCADAMS

STORIES CONSTITUTE
a uniquely powerful currency
IN HUMAN RELATIONSHIPS.

—

-HOWARD GARDNER

THE WORLD OF SOCIAL MEDIA IS ABUZZ
OVER A DESIRE TO CREATE

——

"Social Business"

——

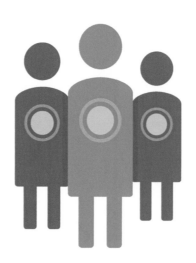

———

"I DON'T HAVE TIME"

"TALK TO ME ABOUT REAL ISSUES, LIKE MARKETING, SELLING"

"I JUST WANT BUSINESS TO GO BACK TO THE WAY IT USED TO BE"

What's Going On Here?

FOR MANY THERE'S AN UNDERLYING ISSUE:

———

BUSINESS AS USUAL DOESN'T FEEL GOOD ANYMORE

———

MISTRUST OF CORPORATIONS AND INSTITUTIONS IS AT EPIC LEVELS (THANK YOU, ENRON). FOR MANY, BUSINESS HAS REPRESENTED PROFIT FOR PROFIT'S SAKE - EVERYTHING ELSE BE DAMNED!

BUSINESS

NEEDS A NEW BRAND STORY

ONE IN WHICH PEOPLE MATTER,
THEIR UNIQUENESS CELEBRATED

BECAUSE WHO WANTS TO DO BUSINESS WITH A FACELESS, SOULLESS ENTITY?

To SUCCEED WE SEEK *relationship.*

WANT A JOB?

ESTABLISH RELATIONSHIPS IN
A NETWORK TO HELP YOU.

WANT TO SELL MORE?

CREATE RELATIONSHIPS WITH CUSTOMERS
BY CONSISTENTLY DELIVERING ON YOUR
PROMISE TO GAIN TRUST.

"OUR SUCCESS HAS
REALLY BEEN BASED ON
partnerships
FROM THE VERY
BEGINNING."

- BILL GATES

"I Love People"

—

"PHYSICAL ATHLETIC ABILITY

IS A DIME A DOZEN

BUT

RELATIONSHIPS ARE

EVERYTHING"

- BILLIE JEAN KING TENNIS CHAMPION, ENTREPRENEUR
AND LEADER FOR SOCIAL CHANGE

THE PARADOX

MOST OF US WERE TAUGHT TO CHECK OURSELVES AT THE OFFICE DOOR

WEARING THE ACCEPTED BUSINESS UNIFORM AND MASK, LEAVING OUR PERSONAL STUFF -EMOTIONS, KNOWLEDGE, RELATIONSHIP, AND STORIES - AT HOME

MANY OF US WOULD BE WELL SERVED TO

RECONNECT WITH *and* SHARE OUR STORIES

ATTRACTING AND BUILDING MEANINGFUL CONNECTION WITH PEOPLE BY SHOWING WE'RE HUMAN AND REAL: LETTING DOWN OUR GUARD, EXPOSING A LITTLE BIT OF VULNERABILITY THAT ALLOWS PEOPLE TO RELATE WITH YOU.

IN AN AUTOMATED, TECHNOLOGY-DRIVEN WORLD

—

IS IT POSSIBLE WE CRAVE *Human Connection?*

People WHO WILL UNDERSTAND OUR SITUATIONS AND HELP US SOLVE OUR PROBLEMS

HUMAN RELATIONSHIP & INTERACTION CAN BRING VALUE & MEANING TO OUR LIVES. REPRESENTING VALUE CREATION AT ITS FINEST.

BUILD TRUST THROUGH *Relationship* WITH PEOPLE

BY FINDING COMMON BONDS AND

CONNECT-ING THE DOTS

A QUICK CONNECTION

B COMMONALITIES

C OPPORTUNITIES

D A FAST TRACK FOR WHY YOU SHOULD CARE

SNAKEOIL SALESMEN

SALESMEN

AND WRITERS OF FICTION

Need Not Apply

———

PEOPLE ARE GOOD AT SNIFFING OUT INSINCERITY.
THEY KNOW WHEN YOU'RE TRYING TO SELL
SOMETHING AND WHEN YOU REALLY CARE. AND
THEY'LL CALL YOU OUT FOR IT BY IGNORING.
DISENGAGING. NOT TRUSTING.

NOT BUYING

& TELLING A VIRAL CHAIN OF FRIENDS

WHO ARE ONLY ONE CLICK AWAY

The New

MARKETING MIX

AND THE ADDITION

OF THE 5TH P:

PEOPLE

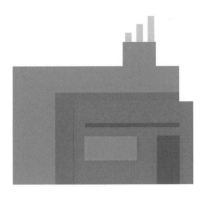

PRODUCT

PLACEMENT

PEOPLE

PROMOTION

PRICE

HIGHLIGHTING A GLARING OMISSION

OF AN OLDER, TRADITIONAL BUSINESS MINDSET
(REMEMBER "PUSH" MARKETING? DOESN'T
SOUND SO INVITING AND HUMAN, DOES IT?)

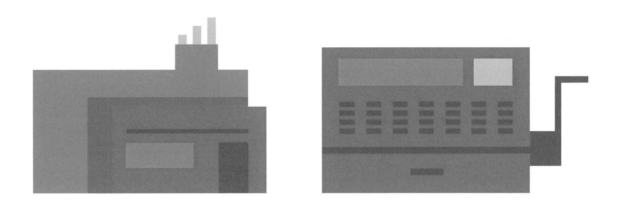

DO YOU REALLY THINK A GREAT PRODUCT & PRICE IS ENOUGH?

PERHAPS WE'RE NOT WELL SERVED BY JUST CARRYING OVER OUR TRADITIONAL WAYS OF THINKING TO THE EMERGING MODELS OF DOING BUSINESS

BEHOLD:

The New
MBA

AN INDICATOR OF THE CHANGING TIMES, THE
WHARTON SCHOOL ANNOUNCED AN OVERHAUL
OF ITS MBA CURRICULUM. WHAT'S NEW: SOFT
SKILLS RELATED TO PEOPLE.

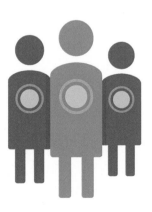

SECTION ⑩

story

(RE)POSITIONS

THE TIMES THEY ARE A-CHANG-ING

- BOB DYLAN

ONE OF THE BEST WAYS TO REINCARNATE IS TO TELL YOUR STORY

- SPALDING GRAY

REPOSITION
REVIVE
REIMAGINE
EVOLVE
REINVENT
RECONNECT

What if DARWIN WAS YOUR BRAND MANAGER?

The EVOLUTION OF YOUR STORY

HOW CAN IT EVOLVE TO RESONATE
IN TODAY'S (AND TOMORROW'S)
WORLD FOR NEW SITUATIONS AND
CHANGING NEEDS?

REINVENTION DOESN'T HAVE TO MEAN

A COMPLETE

Makeover

————

DARWIN'S THEORY: SPECIES BUILD, STRENGTHEN AND EVOLVE FEATURES NECESSARY TO THRIVE IN A GIVEN ENVIRONMENT. INCREMENTAL CHANGES, OVER TIME. ELIMINATING WHAT'S NO LONGER USEFUL

————

THE STORY YOU'VE LIVED IS ONE OF VALUE.
DON'T DISREGARD AND THROW IT AWAY IN
THE NAME OF REINVENTION

PLAY IT FORWARD

RECALIBRATE, RECONNECT AND
GIVE IT NEW MEANING FOR A
NEW ENVIRONMENT

WHAT IT IS:

ADAPTING AND CUSTOMIZING; BUILDING ON YOUR STORY; CREATING A NEW CHAPTER; STAYING TRUE TO WHO YOU ARE; LEVERAGING STRENGTHS

WHAT IT ISN'T:

CHANGING YOUR FACE TIME AND TIME AGAIN; WEARING A MASK; FITTING YOUR BRAND TO SERVE EVERYONE; ACTING; OFF-CHARACTER;

THE BUSINESS PLAN IS DEAD, YOUR STORY IS

Alive

AT BABSON COLLEGE, THE WORLD'S LEADING SCHOOL FOR ENTREPRENEURSHIP, THERE'S A LOT OF TALK ABOUT THE DEATH OF THE BUSINESS PLAN. **AND IT MAKES SENSE: THE MARKET MOVES SO QUICKLY THAT THERE'S LITTLE TIME FOR A START-UP TO SPEND IN A LENGTHY PROCESS OF WRITING. OR AN INVESTOR IN READING.**

INSTEAD, WHAT'S BECOME PREFERRED IS A PROCESS THAT INCLUDES A GREAT IDEA, A SOLID STORY AND A PROCESS OF ACTION & ADJUSTMENT.
A BRAND STORY AND PLAN THAT EVOLVES.

RINSE AND RE-STORY

SELECTIVELY CONSIDER WHICH PARTS OF YOUR STORY ARE RELEVANT FOR YOUR AUDIENCE AND CONTINUOUSLY ADAPT FOR THE SITUATION. BECAUSE YOU'RE ONLY AS GOOD AS YOUR LAST MOVIE.

People Change

THE PEOPLE WHO DEFINE, DELIVER AND INTERACT
WITH YOUR BRAND EVOLVE TOO. ALONG WITH THEIR
PERCEPTIONS, BELIEFS AND NEEDS. ANOTHER REASON TO
MIND THE GAP - UPDATING, EDITING YOUR BRAND STORIES

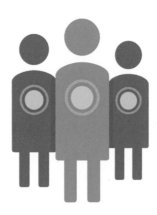

REINVENTING FORD

Getting me to consider the purchase of a Ford is no short order. The odds are stacked against it: I come from a long line of Chevy owners and my great-grandfather owned a dealership during the 1920-30's. My experience with a Ford Escort in the 80's, purchased by my parents, was less than stellar. It got the job done, but I jokingly considered it my tin can on wheels. At the time I believed, like an increasing number of Americans, that the Japanese made Toyota was a better (more reliable, value retaining) purchase. I vowed I'd never buy a Ford.

Imagine my surprise, decades later, to be actually considering and taking a fresh, new look at a Ford. Why? The brand did an amazing job of reconnecting to its original story of quality and value while, at the same time, engaging people through digital media to create a new story — and sense of excitement around the brand. They launched "The Ford Story" on a site dedicated to reconnecting the brand to its original values and playing them forward. And then they created an original and smart campaign to relaunch the one-and-only Ford Fiesta. They selected 100 people representing a new generation of drivers and with strong presence in social media and gave them the European version of the car, 18 months in advance of release in the U.S. The hitch? They had to share their experience on their blogs, Facebook pages, and YouTube channels. This group created a movement — empowered by Ford with the Fiesta as the enabler — of great, personal experiences that were enthusiastically shared. The authenticity of these stories helped establish excitement for — and trust in — the brand with a new generation of drivers.

SECTION ⑪

story
ENGAGES

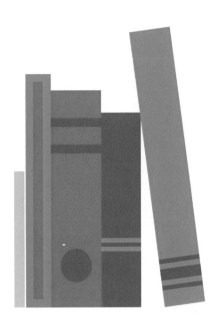

BRAND STORIES ARE

MARKETING & SALES FUEL

BECAUSE TRADITIONAL ADVERTISING IS SO YESTERDAY

ADS ARE BEING SUPPLEMENTED BY

STORY CAMPAIGNS

———

DESIGNED TO CREATE INTEREST IN AND AROUND THE BRAND, WITHOUT OVERTLY SELLING ANYTHING

———

CONTENT IS THE NEW CREATIVE

■ PUTTING FORTH IDEAS, INFO, & RELATED TOPICS OF INTEREST AS THE BASIS OF MARKETING ENGAGEMENT. INVITING PEOPLE INTO CONVERSATION AND EXPERIENCE.

More than

TRADITIONAL

WORD-OF-MOUTH

or testimonials

but IDEAS DESIGNED TO BE

EN-
GAGING

COL-
LABOR-
ATIVE

DISTRIBUTED THROUGH PLATFORMS THAT
Encourage Sharing

GIVING PEOPLE THE
OPPORTUNITY TO HIGHLIGHT

—

THEIR OWN *Stories*

REAL TIME
STORY
DEVELOPMENT

THROUGH CONTENT THAT IS *Compelling*

1. NOT MARKETING MATERIALS IN DISGUISE
2. BUT CONTENT THAT ENTERTAINS, INFORMS, ADVANCES AN IDEA
3. INVITING PEOPLE INTO DISCUSSION AS A MEANS TO CONNECT

The audience chooses to spend time with the story

AND WITH THE BRAND AS WELL

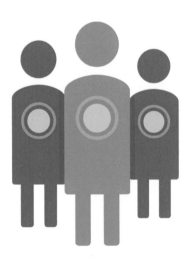

NOBODY CARES ABOUT YOUR COMPANY OR PRODUCT. THEY CARE ABOUT THEIR OWN DREAMS AND GOALS.

———

Help them achieve their aspirations

- HENRY FORD

LEVERAGE THE POWER OF EVERYONE AS A STORYTELLER AND POWERFUL CATALYST FOR YOUR BRAND STORY.

STORY BASED CAMPAIGNS CAN INTEGRATE FAMILIAR CONCEPTS AND VEHICLES:

BLOGS VIDEO FORUMS EVENTS ADVERTISING DISPLAYS

More Content?

—

WE'RE ALREADY BURIED IN INFORMATION

THE BRAND'S NEW ROLE AS

EDITOR

DELIVERING VALUE BY FILTERING STORIES IN A MANNER THAT'S ON MESSAGE, ON BRAND

HELPING TO MAKE SENSE OF MARKET CHAOS THAT CAN RESULT FROM ONGOING CHANGE IN OUR WORLD (MEDIA, TECHNOLOGY AND MORE).

CURATOR & PUBLISHER

AGGREGATING & DELIVERING INFO & IDEAS AROUND A RELATED TOPIC OF INTEREST

ACTING AS A MARKETING AND BIZ DEV TOOL TO ATTRACT AND CONNECT WITH PEOPLE, ESTABLISHING THE BRAND AS TRUSTED, VALUED AND CREDIBLE SOURCE.

DELIVERING

Meaning

HELPING PEOPLE RISE ABOVE THE
MARKET CHAOS TO UNDERSTAND
THE STORIES AT PLAY AND THEIR
IMPLICATIONS FOR BUSINESS.

THERE'S A HIGHER PURSUIT FOR CONTENT MARKETING,
THAT INVOLVES MORE THAN JUST HAVING AN ONLINE
PRESENCE OR CREATING A MOMENT OF IMPACT.

THE ACT OF ONGOING FILTERING &
FOCUS ON MEANINGFUL, RELEVANT
IDEAS CAN HELP
*create community, identify trends, reveal
insight and even solve problems.*

- JAN L. GORDON, FOUNDER OF CURATTI

FILTERING ≠ CONTROLLING

PEOPLE CAN DETECT A SINCERE EFFORT TO DELIVER VALUE AND ENGAGE IN CONVERSATION VERSUS A SELF-SERVING SALES PITCH OR THINLY VEILED PRESS RELEASE/AD. DELIVERING CONTENT OF REAL VALUE WILL SET YOU UP AS CREDIBLE SOURCE AND GIVE PEOPLE A REAL REASON TO ENGAGE AGAIN & AGAIN.

SECTION 12

story
REVEALS

1:1
ENGAGEMENT

CAN BE FACILITATED
BETTER THAN EVER
BEFORE THROUGH

Social Technology

GIVING PEOPLE & BRANDS
UNPRECEDENTED 24/7/365
ACCESS **TO EACH OTHER**

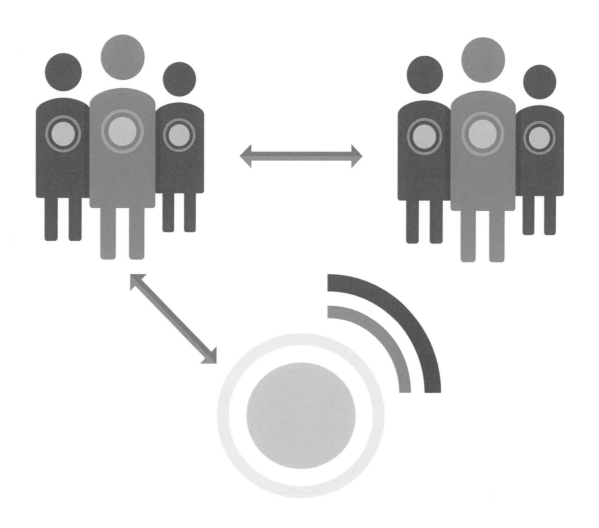

RESEARCH

FUELED BY STORY

Insight:

DISCOVERED THROUGH
PEOPLE'S STORIES
ABOUT YOU.

THROUGH CONVERSATION,
BOTH *direct* AND *indirect.*

THAT CAN INFORM ALL THAT YOU DO:

1. GO-TO-MARKET STRATEGIES

2. PRODUCT DESIGN AND DEVELOPMENT

3. CAMPAIGNS

4. USER EXPERIENCE

5. GROWTH PLANS

6. BRAND DEVELOPMENT

7. POLICIES

THE NEW TOOL: *Story Mining*

ON A DEEP LEVEL, 24/7

INCREASINGLY A RESEARCH

METHODOLOGY OF CHOICE

"Stories do work and so does *Storyworks*. No book will better equip you for the next 10 years in marketing. Read this book, and then go share your stories and build powerful personal, professional and organizational brands"

— Michael Weissman
serial entrepreneur, brand guru and co-author, The Paradox of Excellence

Do you have an idea, product or service that you want to stand out from the crowd? Many of us — as marketers, entrepreneurs and even job hunters — are seeking out the elusive "how to" guidelines for being more than just noticed, but to truly be seen and heard. To have our distinctness and unique value be understood and appreciated.

And, yet, the ability to stand out is getting more and more difficult. The crowd is bigger and noisier than ever, making the need to connect and resonate with people — no matter what you're selling — even more paramount to sustainable success. Yet people are more and more adept at tuning out. Sniffing out — and filtering out — unconvincing and insincere sales pitches.

Want your marketing and sales efforts to be more convincing? This is where story comes into focus. Your story is the special sauce for creating real, meaningful and lasting connection. It provides the antidote to the "tell me about yourself" moment in an interview. And the "so why should I buy from you" response that can create loyalty (not to mention the sale). The beauty: we all think and make sense of the world based on the stories we're told, and the stories we tell ourselves. It's how we operate as people naturally. Using stories provides you with the ability to tap into an established cognitive readiness for your message.

But the impact doesn't end there. Your stories inform your brand and help create more value for your marketing. They are the foundation of organizational culture. And they are the keeper of important insight from your customers, serving as a roadmap toward opportunity and potential.

Storyworks. How Stories Can Advance Your Business, Cause and Career is designed as a primer to help you understand how story — the ones shared by you and others — can help you meet your business objectives and achieve success.

EVERY BRAND HAS A STORY.
ARE YOU PUTTING YOURS TO WORK?

Storyworks is available for special promotions and
premiums. For details call 386.846.8621 or e-mail
sharlene@brandstoria.com

Published 2012 by Brandstoria Press
Alburtis, Pennsylvania
www.brandstoria.com

PRINTED IN THE UNITED STATES OF AMERICA

First Edition: August 2012

ISBN 978-0-6156084-9-5

W W W . B R A N D S T O R I A . C O M

TO MY PARENTS

For driving me all the way to the magic store in Worcester (and listening to me cry all the way home when it was closed). On that day, and countless others, you provided the context for a "you can do it" story that has fueled my dreams and my life. Thank you for your love, care and endless support.

TABLE OF CONTENTS

A Special Thanks

to the brand and organizational storytellers who have offered me a world in which business "makes sense." Especially ANNETTE SIMMONS for writing *The Story Factor*. You: Master. Me: Apprentice. You are the Yoda in my world as a Jedi wannabe (well, my nephews would get that analogy!).

ACKNOWLEDGEMENTS

If it takes a village to raise a child, I'd equate it to be more like a small city-suburb to write a book. My heartfelt thanks and gratitude to all those who've supported me throughout the process:

To my siblings & their families - Paula, Bill & Rachel, Yvonne & Bruce - who put up with me (and regularly feed me).

The Merritts, DeSelms & Monday Night Mayhem crew at Legacy Christian Church for helping me find my place in the One story that really matters.

Janet Greco at the University of Pennsylvania and Transition One Associates who introduced me to the broader role and meaning of story in organizations (and in my life).

My friends, colleagues and frequent coaches: Jon Deutsch, Michael Felberbaum, Jan Gordon, Spence Smith and Cherry Woodburn who have each contributed ideas, feedback and much appreciated encouragement.

Michael Weissman - my Babson College classmate and friend who's hired me, coached me and reminded me of what I love so much about entrepreneurs.

For great design, ideas and problem solving: The Ryans (Smoker and Martin) at The Infantree and Deb Kline. Thank you all for everything you do. And Deb, thank you for your constant source of help. You're a one-of-a-kind treasured friend.

Michael Margolis for encouraging me to find what I "can't stop myself from doing" and for giving me the chance to present at your Reinvention Summit.

My friends for understanding when I was too busy to come out and play. Especially Joe & Sissy: thanks for a great kitchen table "office."

Chuck Brown for generosity, pep talks and faith in me.

Regina Gordin, my University of Pennsylvania classmate and friend who, while studying together in Prague, convinced me that quitting a job wasn't so scary after all. Thank you!

AT THE
HEART
OF SUCCESS

IS A MEANINGFUL CONNECTION TO PEOPLE
AND THEIR STORIES. UNITING THROUGH
EMOTION AND MEANING.

- JANET GRECO, TRANSITION ONE ASSOCIATES

INTRODUCTION

Early in my career as a product manager in the sporting goods industry, I'd think about a product and category in terms of how the customer would receive it in the context of a larger story they held about the brand. If I made a tennis racquet for Spalding, for example, I'd consider: what kind of tennis racquet would people expect from an All-American sports brand known primarily for basketball and golf balls? What would it look like? How would it be priced? This sort of thinking was, I felt, central to the way all product managers considered brand extensions and product development. What I didn't realize, however, was that for many people - managers and customers alike - this was largely a subconcious activity. I was unwittingly leveraging the very way people make sense of the world by tapping into how it informs the potential for a product, service or business.

Many years (brands and products) later, this approach became more solidified and expanded upon through graduate work at the University of Pennylvania where I examined my experience as a manager during the organizational consolidation of five sporting good brands known as Benetton Sportsystem. It had been an exciting and chaotic time working in the throes of organizational change that had left me pondering, during the years that followed, "how could I have better managed and protected the brand?" In my response, I re-discovered the value of story. To people, their identities and their perceived value. At work and in what (and why) they buy.

Storyworks presents the value of story for maximizing your brand -- whether you're a small start up, solo entrepreneur, organizational leader or an individual looking to take the next step in a career. It's designed as a continuous fast read, but one in which you can jump in at any section to discover story's role in helping you achieve a specific objective, such as selling, aligning or engaging. By gaining an understanding of the approach and how it can impact your results, it's my hope that you'll find a new and effective way to make your ideas, initiatives and your businesses a success.

SECTION 1

R.I.P.

FOCUS GROUP

MORE & MORE MARKETERS ARE MOVING
RESEARCH BUDGETS TO SUPPORT ONLINE TOOLS:
ENGAGING IN DIALOGUE AND LISTENING TO
STORIES AS A MEANS OF GATHERING
FEEDBACK & INSIGHT

OUR VISION IN THE MIRROR HAS

Distortion

1. WE COME TO IT WITH ALL OUR BAGGAGE
2. WE'VE GOT ONE EYE ON THE KOOL AID WE'RE DRINKING
3. THE ONE VISIBLE VIEW OFFERS A LIMITED, SINGULAR DIMENSION PERSPECTIVE

"CONSUMERS PRODUCE MORE STORIES THAN WE DO SO LET'S MOVE TOWARD *genuine collaboration*"

WE NEED OTHERS TO OFFER THEIR ONGOING PERSPECTIVE, CONSIDERING THE ROLE THEY PLAY AS CO-CREATORS OF THE BRAND STORY TO MORE FULLY LEVERAGE OPPORTUNITY.

SECTION 13

story
WINS

GIVEN THE CHANGING LANDSCAPE,

MOST OF US ARE REQUIRED TO DO MORE JUST TO SUSTAIN WHAT WE ALREADY HAVE

———

PUT EVERY ASSET YOU HAVE TO WORK

Leverage Your Story

———

ENABLING:

MARKETING CAMPAIGNS THAT WORK

EFFECTIVE LEADERSHIP

IMPROVED NETWORKING

BETTER SEO

STRATEGIES THAT LIVE AND SUCCEED

Artfully

POSITIONING YOUR
BRAND FOR:

OPPORTUNITY
POTENTIAL
SUCCESS

THE AUTHENTICITY

OF OUR STORIES

PROVIDE THE

REAL-LIFE

PROOF AND

SUPPORT

SO, IF YOU REALLY WANT MORE THAN A

MARKETING SHOT IN THE ARM

CONSIDER HOW YOU ACTIVELY CULTIVATE, NURTURE AND DELIVER YOUR STORIES TO REINFORCE AND SUSTAIN YOUR BRAND

MORE MEANINGFUL THAN A CAMPAIGN

——

CREATE, SUPPORT AND LIVE A

Storied Position

AN ACTIVE AWARENESS OF THE EXISTENCE AND IMPACT OF THE STORIES AROUND YOU

NOT AN EITHER-OR PROPOSITION REPLACING THE NEED FOR OTHER ACTIVITIES. OR THE END-ALL FOR EFFECTIVE COMMUNICATIONS AND RELATIONSHIP BUILDING. YOUR STORY'S AN IMPORTANT AND CORE INGREDIENT OF YOUR BRAND, YOUR BUSINESS. AND IT'S WAITING FOR YOU TO LEVERAGE.

Give PEOPLE ANOTHER REASON TO Care.

Resources

Want to learn more? The following resources have served to shape my thinking and provide relevant ideas and frameworks that can impact your business, cause or career:

Scott Bedbury with Stephen Fenichell. (2001). A New Brand World. 8 Principles for Achieving Brand Leadership in the 21st Century. New York: Viking.

The Coca-Cola Company. (2012). Coca-Cola Content 2020. Two part videos created with The Cognitive Media available at http://www.youtube.com/watch?v=LerdMmWjU_E and http://www.cognitivemedia.co.uk/index.php/blog/category/our-work

Stephen M.R. Covey with Rebecca R. Merrill. (2006). The Speed of Trust, The One Thing That Changes Everything. New York: Free Press.

Howard Gardner. (1993). Leading Minds: An Anatomy of Leadership. New York: Basic Books.

Marc Gobé. Emotional Branding. (2001). The new paradigm for connecting brands to people. New York: Allworth Press.

Janet Greco, Ph.D. (1994). Unpublished work from bulkpack from Organizational Dynamics 673, Stories in Organizations: Tools for Executive Development. transitiononeassociates.com

Jim Loehr. (2007). The Power of Story. Rewrite Your Destiny in Business and in Life. New York: Free Press.

Michael Margolis. (2009). Believe Me. A storytelling manifesto for changemakers and innovators. New York: Get Storied Press. getstoried.com

Dan McAdams. (1993). The Stories We Live By. New York: William Morrow.

Robert McKee. (2003). "Stories that moves people: A conversation with a screenwriting coach." Harvard Business Review 81(6):51-55. storylogue.com

Stan Phelps. (2012). What's Your Purple Goldfish. Norwalk, CT: 9 INCH MARKETING, LLC.

Annette Simmons. (2001). The Story Factor. Cambridge, MA: Perseus Publishing. annettesimmons.com

Alan Parry and Robert E. Doan. (1994). Story Re-Visions. Narrative Therapy in the Postmodern World. New York: The Guilford Press.

Raf Stevens. (2011). No Story, No Fans. Build Your Business Through Stories that Resonate. Belgium: dePRESS. www.corporatestoryteller.be

John A. Byrne. Wharton Overhauls MBA Program. Fortune. December 6, 2010. http://management.fortune.cnn.com/2010/12/06/wharton-overhauls-mba-program/

ABOUT THE AUTHOR

Sharlene Sones is a brand-building and marketing specialist that understands the power of a story to sell your product, advance an idea, communicate your value and point the way toward potential.

As Founder of Brandstoria, Sharlene helps entrepreneurs and organizations tap into the heart of their brand. Her approach is rooted in experience launching hundreds of products in sports and entertainment, when she'd think about the strategy for a new product based on its fit with the larger story people held about the brand. Today, she connects this storytelling perspective with traditional branding practices that can surprise and delight in ways that matter.

Over the past decade, Sharlene's worked with and consulted to a wide range of agencies, organizations and global brands including Benetton Sportsystem, Spalding Sports Worldwide, LPGA, Tiffany & Co, University of Pennsylvania, Sigma Designs, IMS Health, Forefront Records, Barnes & Noble Collegiate, Womens Sports Foundation and more.

She's a frequent presenter of workshops and keynotes at conferences including Jeff Pulver's BrandsConf, Reinvention Summit, and The Babson Forum on Entrepreneurship.

When she's not working on someone else's story - she's living out her own in Pennsylvania's beautiful Lehigh Valley, or, as she refers to it, "the deep, deep, deep suburbs of NYC." And while she's put aside a single-engine airplane in favor of a bicycle, you can find Sharlene using power tools: creating something on a wood lathe (Bowl? Pen? Art?) or tackling a DIY home project.

Sharlene earned her graduate degree in organizational dynamics from the University of Pennsylvania and holds a B.S. in management from Babson College, where she serves on the board of the Babson Alumni Association.